An Executive Personal Development Series

Get to the Point

A Short and Snappy Guide

Thejendra Sreenivas

Book Publishing Coach
www.thejendra.com

Copyright © 2026 Thejendra Sreenivas

Second Edition: 2026

All rights reserved. No part of this publication may be reproduced, distributed, or transmitted in any form or by any means, including photocopying, recording, or other electronic or mechanical methods, without the prior written permission of the author or publisher, except in the case of brief quotations embodied in critical reviews and certain other noncommercial uses permitted by copyright law.

Licensing – If you have purchased an eBook or a digital version of this book then it's licensed for your personal enjoyment only. It may not be re-sold or gifted to other people. If you would like to share this with others, please purchase an additional eBook for each person you share it with. If you are reading this and did not purchase it, or it was not purchased for your use only, then please purchase your own copy. Thank you for respecting the publisher's work.

Table of Contents

About the Series iii

Preface v

The Gobbledygook 1

The Risks of Jargon 13

If you are the Communicator 25

If you are the Listener 31

Other Books by the Author.................................... 37

    Author Services 41

About the Author 43

About the Series

The **Executive Personal Development Series** is a set of short non-fiction books on business management, leadership, inspirational, motivational, and self-improvement topics. Each book is an imaginary discussion between a retired professor who thinks unconventionally and a corporate executive who thinks like the crowd. This is a unique professor who thinks, "*What is popular may not be right, and what is right may not be popular.*"

Most self-help books are normally written in a textbook or step-by-step guide formats. But these books are written like a novel in a conversational style with interactive lectures, candid arguments, and idle talk between the two who belong to different generations. Each book discusses some self-improvement concept or an aspect of the executive's personal or professional life and the professor enlightens, alters, or completely demolishes the executive's earlier thinking and assumptions.

The first book in the series is **The Power of**

Laziness followed by **The Extreme Minimalist** and others. However, each book can be read independently.

Preface

Have you ever felt that you have fallen under the toxic spell of modern business jargon? Are you bombarded by an endless stream of corporate mumbo-jumbo? Are you going bald scratching your head trying to understand complex reports filled with meaningless words like synergy, value-add, leverage, paradigm, core competency, catalyst, vision, mission, information-centric, people-oriented, horizontal and vertical solutions, and other gobbledygook? Are you tolerating and encouraging fools by mistaking their pretentious rubbish talk for intelligence?

If you say yes to any or all of the above questions, then you are not alone. Millions of executives worldwide are in the same situation and have resigned themselves to fate, unable and unwilling to get out of it. But it need not be that way. You can get out of it easily if you are willing to do a few simple things. This book will show you those simple things, and how you can consciously reject complexity in communication and hug simplicity, which is the ultimate sophistication.

Happy Reading

The Gobbledygook

After completing the two amazing workshops on laziness and minimalism, I became a regular visitor to the professor's lectures as I was now determined to exploit all his wonderful knowledge. Each time I visited him, I learned something new that altered or demolished my previous way of thinking and assumptions. He was also happy that he had found a student like me who had the time and patience to listen to his point of view. We would often have candid debates on many things, and the professor had an endless supply of unusual topics to discuss and debate. Today, when I visited him, he seemed excited to meet me. I suspected that he had discovered a new topic to enlighten me, or something was troubling him.

"Got any new business topics to fight, professor?" I joked.

"Yes, yes, I was reading a few brochures on some company products and services that made me dizzy and thought this would be a good topic for us to debate."

"Good, what's it about?"

"I will tell you, but first let me ask you a question. If a caveman sees a saber-toothed tiger approaching his cave, how exactly should he communicate this horror to his wife and kids?

Should he scream, RUN AND HIDE!!!

Or should he say,

Folks, I see an immediate threat from a ferocious creature seeking palatable items to fulfill his non-negotiable needs, which poses a serious danger and disruption to all of us. It is imperative that we take immediate action to mitigate the grave risk by urgently harnessing the power of our legs.

"Which statement would have communicated the message better to his family?"

"Obviously, Run and Hide. Why would he use that long gibberish sentence?"

"Well, back in the Stone Age, the first sentence (Run and Hide) would have obviously produced the necessary results. But in our modern times, especially in your business world, such a plain and simple sentence would be immediately considered a highly unacceptable communication."

"Huh, why is it unacceptable?"

"My dear fellow, it's unacceptable because it is simple and easy to understand."

"I don't get your point. What's wrong with simplicity, professor?"

"Well, simplicity is a big NO-NO in today's corporate world. It is a taboo, a career roadblock, and you will be branded as a corporate simpleton if you use simplicity."

"Why is that? I don't understand what you are trying to say."

"Even I don't understand what you corporate folks say and write nowadays. This is why I did a bit of brainstorming over the last few days and thought it would be good to attack your modern corporate communication specialists."

"Why would you want to attack our corporate communication specialists? What wrong did they do?"

"I feel they need to be attacked and educated about communications."

"Educated about communications? What new things will you teach them about communications?"

"I was thinking of teaching them some fundamentals of communications."

"Teach them fundamentals? Well, professor, most of these specialists have a Diploma or Master's degree in communications. Why would you want to teach them fundamentals?"

"Well, sometimes the student has to teach the master. Education cannot always be a one-way street."

"Okay, please explain your puzzle."

"Today, the word 'communication' is a common buzzword in all business environments worldwide. Secondly, the need for effective communication has become a top priority for all business leaders. Hence, organizations worldwide are spending millions of dollars every year on corporate communications, which happen in the form of team meetings, intranets, brochures, speeches, emails, slide presentations, workshops, executive retreats, video presentations, etc. As an employee at any level, you would have definitely attended (or conducted) heaps of communication sessions on various business or customer issues. Naturally, you will agree that a lot of effort, time, and money are required for such activities. However, despite so much effort on communications, it's still a frightening and terrifying beast for most employees to handle."

"Why do you say so?"

"To understand why, just answer a couple of questions honestly. First question. For example, you read a modern company product or service brochure, a corporate communication slideshow, a strategy, or a business proposal from head to toe, and then you read it again and perhaps again. But, internally, you get a feeling that you are simply reading the words without any meaningful information entering your brain. Have you experienced this weird feeling?"

"Hey, you are right!"

"Second question. Or in some cases, you attend a flashy business presentation, a seminar, or a business speech by a top management guru or a modern flashy CEO that probably lasts for an hour. You remember walking in with a lot of hope and anticipation, but always end up walking out blank, confused, and unable to remember anything the speaker spoke for more than an hour. After it's over, you begin to secretly think, 'I don't understand. What was the speaker talking about? What exactly do I need to do?' But you feel embarrassed to ask anyone for clarification or more details. You may also begin to wonder if there is something wrong with your brain for being unable to understand what was being said. Or you think the stuff they were presenting is too advanced and beyond your humble capabilities, and perhaps not for ordinary mortals. Have you experienced these uncomfortable feelings?"

"Yes, you are right again."

"So why was it fuzzy to you? Where exactly is the problem? Or was it fuzzy to everyone?"

"Hmm, I am not sure about everyone. But I do get confused in such flashy business seminars."

"The answer is, you are not alone."

"Really?"

"You may be surprised to know that worldwide millions of employees experience the same confusion and fuzziness as you do in every modern workplace every day, but are simply too embarrassed or even scared to admit it. If you are one such employee in any workplace, then I suggest you stop worrying or feeling embarrassed about your situation. Frankly, there is nothing wrong with you, as we shall shortly see. And there is no need to visit any brain surgeon or psychiatrist or refresh your grammar. The problem does not lie with you. The culprit is actually business jargon."

"What's business jargon?"

"A general dictionary defines jargon as, 'Unintelligible or meaningless talk or writing, gibberish. Any talk or writing that one does not understand.' And business jargon is the art of talking (or writing) about various business issues using complicated and confusing words. To see how jargon has invaded all areas of your corporate and even personal lives, let me give some examples."

"Okay."

"**Example-1:** Just visit any business website and you will definitely see plenty of meaningless colorful words, self-congratulatory sentences, and lots of self-trumpeting about their products, services, and the special breed of vibrant people they have. Words like synergy, value-add, core, catalyst, vision, mission, information-centric, people-oriented, horizontal and vertical solutions, etc., are commonly and generously used in every brochure, presentation, website, speech, etc., to give the audience an impression of superiority and dazzle the customer.

Example-2: If you want to buy any product, or service, pay a bill, or seek an answer from any company website these days it's nearly impossible for you to get the required essential details like specifications, cost, etc., quickly without first wading through several kilometers of jargon describing how great the company is, its fantastic ever smiling people, their immense passion for serving you and so on.

Example-3: Look at the kind of complex modern sentences used nowadays to describe simple things.

Simple
I am going on a sales call.
Complex
I am trying to widen our customer base to improve the company's bottom line.

Simple
It's too costly to buy and maintain.
Complex
The financial factors relating to the product procurement & associated implementation coupled with the ROI factors currently do not allow us to proceed further.

Simple
We will make a loss this year due to poor sales.
Complex
Due to unpredictable market conditions, external competitiveness, and a saturated customer base coupled with corrections in our profit predictions,

our revenues will be on the decline. Some negative figures are expected.

Simple
We need to work hard to improve business.
Complex
We need to enhance our core competitiveness to adapt to increasing competition for sourcing new customers.

Simple
It's suitable if you plan to use it for a short time.
Complex
It's suitable to use it in the interim, till a long-term solution is available.

Simple
When will our machine get repaired?
Complex
We would like to know the estimated timeframe for this equipment downtime is going to interrupt our main business.
Simple
Is this product useful?

Complex

We would like to know what intangible benefits and values this product would add to our core business.

Simple

Since you know how to operate this product can you teach a few others?

Complex

You need to demonstrate the usability of this product to other resources to enhance our knowledge management database for efficient information dissemination.

"Had enough?"

"Wow! You have collected plenty of examples, professor. I never thought of communications in this way."

"This usage of jargon is the root cause of miscommunication and confusion in most modern organizations."

"Okay, if jargon is such a problem, why do companies use it?"

"Well, here are a few reasons."

Reason 1: Business executives believe that complexity gives them an aura of security and superiority. This is why most business leaders these days are rejecting simplicity and making things complex by using business jargon. Hence, most businesses today deliberately avoid easy and simple words when they want to convey any message. Instead, they use all kinds of complex, complicated, and meaningless words in the hope of impressing their audiences with their superior intellect.

Reason 2: Secondly, marketing studies have shown that many customers and competitors can be easily fooled and made to pay more if high-sounding words can be used to describe their products and services. This is based on a timeless cheating principle that says, if you can't convince them, confuse them. This concept is a very convenient way for companies to show off to gullible customers that they are selling something unique or revolutionary, even if they are selling something as simple as a toothpick or a safety pin. For example, people are willing to pay a ransom for an Apple iPhone just because of the glamour and hype surrounding it, even though there are better phones with superior specs at much lower costs.

Reason 3: Organizations today are fiercely competing with one another even though they may be selling similar products and services. It's a daily business war. Now how can one wage the competition war and lure customers their way? Simple, they start adding generous doses of jargon to their products and services to make customers believe that they are selling something unique that no one else is doing. For example, look at two companies that sell almost identical products like smartphones or cars. If you read their product specifications and marketing hype, you will be amazed at the kind of fancy words they use to claim that their product is the best, even though both competitor products may have almost identical specifications."

"Hmm, you are right, professor."

"This is enough for today. We shall discuss the risks of jargon tomorrow."

The Risks of Jargon

"What risks can jargon have, professor?"

"Jargon may seem harmless and even amusing, but it has many hidden dangers. The harm that jargon can cause may not be immediately obvious to everyone, but it can have a corrosive effect on companies and individuals and cause more problems than a total lack of communication."

"How?"

"To see how, just listen to my lecture on the kinds of problems that jargon and hype can create. Interrupt me if you need any clarifications."

Message gets lost: As stated earlier, organizations and business leaders these days fear plainness, and that is why they try to make things complex by using business jargon, complex words, and so on. They try to dazzle their audience with high-sounding words, colorful presentations, and all sorts of gimmicks in the hope of doing effective communications. But they usually end up doing exactly the opposite, which is ineffective communication, confusion, and brainwashing of the audience. When colorful language and complicated words are used, the real message gets lost or buried so deep that no one can understand it. There will be plenty of talk, but no clear message. Secondly, it bores and confuses the listener. In many cases, the message gets twisted out of shape, can convey different meanings to different people, and can lead to reading between the lines to spread rumors. Customers and employees will not be able to ask appropriate questions or cannot ask any questions at all because nothing is clear. Or a few smart ones will ask some more jargon-filled questions to get some more jargon-filled answers. But it only makes things complicated and does not serve its purpose.

No going back: Once companies bite the jargon bug, it's very difficult to come out. It will become like the Emperor's new clothes story, where no one is willing to say that the king is naked. And nobody will dare bell the cat. Soon, complexity is adored, worshipped, and organizations behave as if every employee has been hypnotized by some mysterious force to shun simplicity. This results in every modern business suffering from complicated project plans, ridiculous mission and vision statements, complex paperwork, tedious procedures, cumbersome business transformations, jargon-spewing executives, etc., that engulf everything right from the janitor's department to the CEO's office. Even the most trivial of tasks are made difficult and daunting. In layman's terms, modern business is like walking through thick smoke or a business fog, unable to see the path clearly. This fog turns every employee into a living zombie who becomes oblivious to the pain of complexity. Unfortunately, the complexity you see has evolved over the years due to many sane and insane reasons and keeps growing by the day.

Confuses employees: When hit by complexity and business jargon, most employees will be afraid to ask for specifics due to the fear of being branded as simpletons. Secondly, without realizing jargon is the root cause of miscommunication, employees in most modern organizations mistakenly complain there is no communication at all from their management. But there is actually enough communication happening all around to drown you to the depths of the earth. In fact, and to be fair, business managements today do take enormous pains and effort in dumping truckloads of communication on their employees, shareholders, company websites, brochures, advertisements, etc. But what is clearly lacking is a truly simple and easy-to-understand message from the communicator that everyone in the intended audience can understand without misinterpreting. So, when employees complain there is a lack of communication, they actually mean the information is not available in a manner that a layman can understand. For example, a commonly used business statement and phrase like, "We deliver superior value and competitive advantage by focusing on our core competencies," has no clear meaning, or it can mean different things to different people.

Attracts liars and cheats: Jargon is often the backdoor for liars, cheats, and hollow people to enter organizations. For example, assume two candidates apply for a position in an organization. The normal method is to interview the candidate based on the resume they submit. Now suppose one candidate has a simple and straightforward resume, while the other submits a fancy one with lots of colorful words and sentences that trumpet and glorify the routine (or even mediocre) work done in his previous job. In all probability, the candidate with a fancy resume will be able to easily clinch the job with his or her choice of words that can impress the interviewer. Hype and jargon can portray a false picture that the candidate has a keen grasp of the big picture, is an excellent leader, a supreme intellectual, etc. For example, a fancy sentence like, "I was the key leader and catalyst for enhancing customer-centric business landscapes," stated in a pompous manner, can make the interviewer fall off his chair mesmerized. But the actual work in all probability will not be rocket science or something that ordinary mortals cannot do or learn. However, the other candidate who tries to explain his work in ordinary and real-world terms will definitely lose his chance for the job, as he will be classified as a non-enterprising simpleton, while the bogus chap will get selected as a great leader.

Job ads become scary: Look at the kind of scary job advertisements these days even for the simplest of jobs. For example, just look at the kind of internal and external advertisements you see in newspapers or job-related websites. They will be dripping in jargon like below:

We are looking for high-value employees dedicated to delivering constant innovation to assist our clients in high-performance delivery and meet our strategic goals.

The employee must be a class of his own and raise his or her sights above the horizon. He or she must be a people leader who has the challenge to outdo themselves and be a global winner all the way to confidently swim in an ocean of opportunities.

We are looking for super-efficient leaders who have the challenge to outdo themselves and be a winner all the way.

We are looking for a person to lead, motivate, and create a high-performance team capable of continuous innovation and excellence in working for a global leader.

We are looking for candidates who are bubbling, energetic, and invigorating to join a sales team of global winners.

"Don't the ads look scary?"

"Definitely, professor."

"Where do you find such people? How many such supermen and superwomen have you seen in your own organization, in your family, or in society around? Secondly, even though the above ads are scary, in reality, the actual jobs will be nothing extraordinary and will fall under the standard jobs like managerial, sales, marketing, technical, finance, legal, etc. But such hyped ads will prevent honest people from applying for such jobs. This is because honest and knowledgeable people applying to such positions will feel, 'Oh my god, they are expecting to hire some fancy rocket scientist who can innovate daily! I don't think I can do that.' So, organizations end up hiring liars, cheats, bogus people, and hot-air specialists."

"Hot air? Why do you say so?"

"It's because of fancy titles executives nowadays have. Have you observed the kind of fancy titles that employees nowadays have in offices, or call themselves on their LinkedIn profiles or other websites? For example, a supervisor or manager can now call himself or herself a Chief Value Creator, Evangelist, Solution Provider, Talent Guru, Enabler, Catalyst, Innovator, Visionary, Customer Experience Enhancer, Creativity Enhancer, Thought Leader, Influencer, Wizard, etc. What do these pompous titles mean? What kind of amazing activities will they do daily? Are all their ideas and suggestions awesome? Have you seen such geniuses in your organization? Do you think they will be laying golden eggs every day? In reality, there will be nothing special about them or the job they do to be called by such fancy titles. Remember, the actual work people do is quite different from the bogus and fancy job descriptions associated with it. In summary, this is another example of how lying and glorifying their routine and ordinary jobs becomes the norm."

"Hmm."

Financial disasters: Jargon and high-sounding names have also played an important role in the collapse of many financial institutions worldwide, the creation of the subprime crisis, etc., that happened in 2008. Many banks and financial institutions created highly risky investments using cool, fancy names and sold them to gullible investors worldwide. Because of the sophistication they used, it gave such financial carrots an aura of credibility and security. Hence, many investors, even intelligent ones, were taken for a ride as they could not fully understand what a mess they were getting into. However, if simple, understandable language was used, then many people could have taken necessary precautions, and a lot of unnecessary financial ruin and destruction of families could have been avoided.

Jargon corrupts everyone: Business jargon is not only confusing and misleading, but it is also very contagious. If you work in any modern organization, you will soon start talking and writing hot air. You can no longer speak plain English. It is like if you smell shit long enough, you will begin to like it. Once jargon and hype become the standard in an organization, it will no longer be possible for any employee or department to conduct meetings, seminars, presentations, etc., without the necessary dosages of colorful words and gibberish. You soon become terrified of simplicity. And anyone who uses ordinary words or refuses to join the language insanity will be classified as a simpleton who will not be suitable for managing large teams, big projects, dealing with the top brass, and so on.

Delay and money: You can't shoot a target you can't see. Similarly, you can't do what you don't understand. Organizational decision-making and speed suffer, as even the most trivial of reports, proposals, decisions, and output get delayed because they do not contain the necessary dosages of jargon and cosmetics. So, organizations waste time, money, and effort in trying to meet each other's expectations and requirements that are not available in easy, simple-to-use language."

"Yes, yes, that simple language is missing nowadays, professor."

"Now let's look at some popular jargon and what they actually mean."

- Touch Base Offline – This means let's meet and talk.
- Blue Sky Thinking – Give ideas without any constraints.
- Think Outside the Box – Means think creatively.
- It's on my Radar – Which means I am aware of this.
- Become a Change Agent – Lead whatever change without grumbling.
- Get on All Fours – Look at something in full detail.
- Take it to Next Level – Make it better.
- Low Hanging Fruit – Something that doesn't require much effort.
- Not enough Bandwidth – Too busy to do more work.
- Helicopter View – Have a broad view of some issue or project.
- Boil the Ocean – Do the impossible.

- Idea Shower – Meet and share ideas for something.
- Peel the Onion – Examine in detail.
- We will Park that – We will not discuss it now.
- This idea won't scale – I hate this idea.
- Pick your brain – Ask a few questions.
- Let's Circle Back Later – Let's see later.
- Reach out – Talk to him or her.
- Though Leader – Knows how to think.
- Connect the Dots – Link them.

"Hmm, you are right. Not everyone can understand this jargon. So, what can I do to make my communication simple and effective?"

"Essentially, the key to effective communication is straightforwardness and the use of simple words, even if it is unpopular. Winston Churchill, one of the most straightforward leaders history has ever produced, would say, 'If you have an important point to make, don't try to be subtle or clever. Use a pile driver. Hit the point once. Then come back and hit it again. Then hit it a third time—a tremendous whack.' This should be your approach to communication, though you may not need a pile driver at all times. For communication to occur, two parties are required. One is the person saying or writing something, and the other is the person listening or reading it. Depending on who you are at the moment, you can do your bit to avoid jargon and make the communication clear. We shall discuss that tomorrow."

If you are the Communicator

"Today we shall discuss how you should communicate if you are the communicator."

"Okay."

"Your message will be clearly heard only if you use plain language and simple words that people can remember. So, ask yourself whether you genuinely intend to convey the message and communicate, or you just want to impress others with your keen grasp of colorful and complicated words. Business jargon has been a laughing matter for years and will make you look like a bogus person. Just because you are a senior person does not mean you have to use complicated words to get something done. Remember, juniors, newcomers, and spectators will not openly tell you they did not understand anything, but will laugh at you behind your back.

There is nothing to be ashamed of if you use simple words. Remember, if a million people say a foolish thing, it is still a foolish thing. So, just because every businessman you know or see talks gibberish, you don't have to join the bandwagon to survive. And in case you are just a postman conveying someone's message, first make sure you have clearly understood what is to be said so that you don't pass the wrong message. Learn to get to the point like the mythical swan."

"What mythical swan?"

"In Hindu mythology, there is a concept called the Hamsa-Ksheera Nyaya, which is to be like a mythical swan (hamsa) for its uncanny ability to suck only milk (ksheera) from a mixture of milk and water (neera). Milk stands for essence (simplicity) and water stands for the useless (complexity). Ask yourself, do you talk like that at home or with your neighbors and relatives? Can you really talk like that at home? Unless it is confidential, print a copy of your corporate communication pack and show it to your mom or grandma and ask if they can understand what is written. If they say, 'Duh!!!' then you get the point. Employees avoid managers and leaders who talk gibberish. So, become a go-to person that ordinary people can connect with and who is approachable for help and advice.

Today, people already suffer from information overload and hype. They don't want more of such stuff and crave simplicity. If you want to convey the message, then you should be straight and simple, like Reagan used to talk. For example, during the Cold War era, President Reagan told Gorbachev, 'General Secretary Gorbachev, if you seek peace, if you seek prosperity for the Soviet Union and Eastern Europe, if you seek liberalization: Come here to this gate! Mr. Gorbachev, open this gate! Mr. Gorbachev, tear down this wall.' He was referring to the Berlin Wall that divided East and West Germany. He did not beat around the bush with empty words like many diplomats do.

Mass advice: Nowadays it has become a norm for many famous CEOs and top managers to frequently give flamboyant jargon-filled speeches to their global audience. Such speeches are normally telecast worldwide via their internal network or through the internet. The business media will also add spice to such speeches or initiate further interviews, etc. The internet has hundreds of such videos from many Fortune 500 companies. But if you observe closely, such mass speeches will hardly contain any meaningful or useful information. To know why, let's play a small game. For example, assume you are a jargon-loving CEO or a senior manager of a large organization and you gave a grand motivational speech to your worldwide staff (with diverse departments and age groups) and used sentences like: Reach for the stars, Conquer new kingdoms, Demolish hierarchy, Break all the rules, Thrill the customer, Add value, Act empowered, Connect the dots, Break all barriers, Do what is right, etc. Now, what exactly are your employees at all layers supposed to do from tomorrow after listening to your advice?

Can they start ignoring their HR policies to break the rules?

Take decisions without their manager's approval to demonstrate empowerment?

Stop downsizing because it's not right?

Give massive discounts to customers to thrill them and add value?

Make everyone's titles the same to demolish hierarchy?

Invade other departments to break all barriers?

Will you or your senior managers allow them to do it, though you enthusiastically preached it?"

And so on.

"No way, professor."

"Obviously no. So, any mass advice with jargon just pumps up people for a short time, but the advice can't really be followed and can mean different things to different people. Does this mean all motivational talk is useless? The answer is Yes and No. Unless there is a clear real-world takeaway from the advice you give, just using a lot of fancy words, waving your hands, and mesmerizing your audience accomplishes nothing other than them being dazzled by you for an hour. This is enough for today. Tomorrow we shall discuss some more points."

If you are the Listener

"Today we shall discuss what you can do if you are the listener."

"Okay."

"Jargon is mainly used by senior executives and management gurus. You will very rarely hear junior employees speaking jargon. As a listener or a recipient, you need to think about what choices you have to accept or prevent jargon. Here are a few methods you can use to eliminate or reduce the harmful effects of jargon.

Method 1: If you are sitting and listening to a flamboyant business speech, then jargon may not personally impact you much. You can forget about it as soon as the speech gets over. However, with one-on-one discussions with customers, bosses, supervisors, etc., you should never accept jargon without asking probing questions that will give you a realistic picture of what needs to be done. When something appears complex, don't be afraid to ask elementary questions, dumb questions, or even absurd questions. If you know the subject matter well and it still appears complex, then don't portray an illusion of understanding. Don't nod your head when a customer says he needs value addition month-on-month to meet his strategic objectives. Ask what he means by that through some examples. Don't try to read his mind to know what he wants. Is he willing to pay for higher services? In all probability, he won't be able to explain clearly, nor afford what it involves to get what he wants.

Different people understand the same thing from different angles. So, cultivate a "Show me how or let me do it" habit. Think of hypothetical situations where you have to do everything yourself or teach everything to someone else. Peter Drucker once said, 'My greatest strength as a consultant is to be ignorant and ask a few simple questions.' So, become a Drucker and ask simple questions, even dumb ones if necessary for better clarification. Do not hesitate to state you did not understand something. Dumb questions are better than making false and wrong assumptions that lead to disastrous end results.

Method 2: Not accepting jargon may not be possible, as it's mainly used by senior executives and management gurus. If it's just some general advice, you can probably ignore it as nobody will remember it two hours later. In all probability, the communicator will not be able to repeat the exact same sentence again if it was filled with jargon. But if there is real work to be done, then you will need clear information to start. So, if you are dumped with jargon, you should try to rephrase it into simple terms and ask the teller, 'This is what I understood. Correct me if I am wrong.'

Method 3: Learn to recognize when you are being bombarded by jargon. Remember one thing: unless you are not paying attention, communication is all about understanding the message right by the intended audience in a manner everyone can fully understand. For example, a botanist can talk a simple sentence mixed with biology terms, which you may not understand. That is understandable and cannot be called bad communication. But if you know the subject well and still can't understand even when paying attention, then it is dripping with jargon.

Somebody once jokingly said, 'In the real world there is no such thing as algebra.' Similarly, in reality, there is no need for unnecessary business jargon. Hence, it is necessary to distinguish between reality and hype in the workplace, especially to avoid stress and anxiety chasing hype and hot air. If jargon is getting you down, be firm and say that you are unable and unwilling to understand the jargon and colorful language.

Method 4: Learn to separate the wheat from the chaff. Be like an elephant. It has been said elephants can detect the slightest amount of unusual noise among the countless noise and din created by other animals around. Similarly, you should learn to suck only the essence and filter out all complexity. Remember, if a million people do a foolish thing, it is still a foolish thing. Often you can reduce any project, no matter how big or complicated, into a simple short summary that contains all the necessary details to take a correct decision. For example, a fifty-page report may really contain only ten to fifteen pages of useful information that is needed to make a decision, while the remaining forty-five pages could just be cosmetics, bells, and whistles.

Method 5: Learn to know the difference between difficulty and complexity. Few people realize that difficulty is different from complexity. Difficulty is a natural thing based on the task and depends on the effort involved. But complexity is a man-made thing, an aura of hype deliberately invented to make the task look glamorous, impress others, and separate the royals from the commoners. Difficulty is unavoidable, but complexity is optional. Many business decisions, even billion-dollar ones, can be easily taken if one has the realistic experience to summarize them into a few pages containing the absolute essential details. But if it's mandatory to go through the rigmarole of a "one method fits all" flamboyant process of fancy presentations, endless meetings, status reports, jargon-filled complex paperwork outlining all the unwanted and unviable alternatives, etc., then the same decision now becomes complicated and tedious.

Method 6: If a million people say a foolish thing, it does not automatically become a wise thing. It's still a foolish thing. And what is popular may not be right, and what is right may not be popular. Jargon is garbage and crap, no matter how popular it may be. So, don't be afraid to be plain and straightforward in the fog of complex business jargon. Don't become a fake due to peer pressure or to avoid criticism. Do not be overwhelmed by hot air and flamboyance. You must ruthlessly reject complexity, jargon, hot air, and other modern ailments without hesitation or embarrassment and seek simplicity in everything. If you are unable or unwilling to reject complexity, then it can create unnecessary stress, anxiety, and confusion. It's only when things are easy that you can achieve greatness, speed, and clarity. Plainness is less trouble and you won't be wasting time chasing mirages. Hence, insist on simplicity even if it makes you appear simplistic. The essence of all advanced knowledge is simplicity and clarity. Finally, we can conclude my lecture with a quote from Leonardo da Vinci, who said, 'Simplicity is the ultimate sophistication.'

"This means we complete another amazing workshop, professor. I wonder what terrific topic you will think of next."

Other Books by the Author

Personal Planner

Personal Disaster Preparedness Planner
Organize your Information, Belongings, and Activities to Protect your Family in a Crisis

Humor Books

Become a Dictator
A Short and Snappy Guide

Become a Modern Artist
The Greatest and Easiest Job on Earth

Big Money
Top Secret Guide to the Stock Market Circus

The Mirage Peddlers
How to Become an Advertising Guru

The Mud Horse
Fantastic Jobs for Firebrand Feminists

Spirituality Books

The Miracle Law
The Pristine Path to Purpose and Prosperity

The Inventor of Nothing
A Mild and Wild Chat with the Brilliant Cosmic Designer

Personal Development Books

The Power of Laziness
Discovering the Wisdom of Slowness

The Extreme Minimalist
Discovering the Joys of Minimalism and Frugality

Get to the Point
A Short and Snappy Guide

The Curses of a Thousand Mothers
How We Pursue Joyful Sins

The Long Fuse
Why the Buddha Never Took Aspirin

No Easy Future!
Seven Habits to Tackle Tomorrow

The Compass Mind
A Short Guide to Think in All Directions

Start Saying NO!
How to Stop Living for Others and Start Pursuing your Goals

The Gibraltar Briefcase
The Wise Weapons of Exceptional Executives

The Glass Prison
The How to Stay Productive during a Lockdown

Children Books

Secret Trip to a Jolly Jungle
The Adventures of Tommy and his Magic Spaceship

Secret Trip into the Ocean
The Adventures of Tommy and his Magic Spaceship

Secret Trip to a Treasure Island
The Adventures of Tommy and his Magic Spaceship

Secret Trip to Outer Space
The Adventures of Tommy and his Magic Spaceship

The Magic Apple and his Mighty Friends

Technology Books

IT Asset Management
A Practical Guide for Technical and Business Executives

Disaster Recovery and Business Continuity
A Quick Guide for Organizations and Business Managers

Practical IT Service Management
A Concise Guide for Busy Executives

Fiction Books

FINK!
The Mafia's Nightmare

The Patriot's Confession
A Spy Thriller

The World's Shortest Novels
The Sixty Seconds Bookshelf

Personal Development Magazine
Wealth of the Wise

All the above books are available in both Paperback and eBook on all major book retailers

Author Services

Become an Author Course - Do you dream of becoming an Author? Do you want to share your Knowledge, Imagination, or Experience and write your first Fiction or Non-Fiction Book? Then take my Self-Paced Video Course on Thinkific for just US$79.95. The link is below.

https://thejendra.thinkific.com/courses/how-to-become-an-author-and-self-publish-your-book

Publish your Book Project - If you have already written a book and want to publish it, then I can help you to Self-Publish it Worldwide on Amazon, Apple, Kobo, BN, Google Play, Flipkart, and other book retailers in both Paperback and all eBook formats through my unique Assisted Self Publishing method.

Visit http://www.author-world.com for details

About the Author

Good day. My name is **Thejendra Sreenivas**. I was a Technology Manager in the IT industry for nearly 30 years. Before entering the IT industry, I was also an electronics lecturer for a short duration.

I have written and self-published 35+ books on various subjects. All my books are available in both Paperback and Kindle on Amazon and as an eBook on Apple, Kobo, B&N, Google Play, and many other retailers. I am also the Editor and Publisher of a font-optimized digital magazine called **Self Improvement International** which contains articles on personal development, workplace issues, humor, writing, and publishing.

I am now a **Book Publishing Coach** and offer services like *Assisted Self-Publishing, Manuscript Formatting, Facebook Ads, Ghostwriting, One Page Websites, Article Writing, and Podcast Creation*. In addition, I also offer Personal Development Coaching.

Please visit my web cave - **www.thejendra.com** or **www.author-world.com** for details of my books, magazine, and coaching information.

Online Courses by the Author

www.ingramcontent.com/pod-product-compliance
Lightning Source LLC
Chambersburg PA
CBHW021044180526
45163CB00005B/2273